ITALIAN LACE DESIGNS
243 Classic Examples

Elisa Ricci

DOVER PUBLICATIONS, INC.
New York

Copyright

Copyright © 1993 by Dover Publications, Inc.
All rights reserved under Pan American and International Copyright Conventions.

Published in Canada by General Publishing Company, Ltd., 30 Lesmill Road, Don Mills, Toronto, Ontario.
Published in the United Kingdom by Constable and Company, Ltd., 3 The Lanchesters, 162–164 Fulham Palace Road, London W6 9ER.

Bibliographical Note

Italian Lace Designs: 243 Classic Examples, first published by Dover Publications, Inc., in 1993, is a new selection of photographs from *Old Italian Lace, Volumes I and II* by Elisa Ricci, published by William Heinemann, London, and J. B. Lippincott Company, Philadelphia, in 1913. A new Publisher's Note has been written for this edition.

DOVER *Pictorial Archive* SERIES

Library of Congress Cataloging-in-Publication Data

Ricci, Elisa.
    Italian lace designs : 243 classic examples / Elisa Ricci.
        p.   cm. — (Dover pictorial archive series)
    ". . . new selection of photographs from 'Old Italian lace, volumes I and II' by Elisa Ricci, published by William Heinemann, London, and J.B. Lippincott Co., Philadelphia in 1913"—copr. p.
    ISBN 0-486-27588-4 (pbk.)
    1. Lace and lace making—Italy—Themes, motives. I. Ricci, Elisa. Old Italian lace. II. Title.
III. Series.
NK9452.A1R53 1993
746.2'2'0945—dc20
                                                     93-16990
                                                        CIP

Manufactured in the United States of America
Dover Publications, Inc., 31 East 2nd Street, Mineola, N.Y. 11501

PUBLISHER'S NOTE

L ACE HAS A LONG AND ROMANTIC, if somewhat shrouded, history. Just exactly when and where it developed is a matter of some controversy, but that Italy produced some of the most beautiful laces ever known is disputed by few.

"True" lace can be divided into two major classifications—needlepoint lace and bobbin lace. Needlepoint lace, as the name implies, is worked with a needle and a single thread. Bobbin lace is made by interweaving many threads together. It is unclear which type developed first, but both types were well established by the sixteenth century.

One of the earliest forms of openwork was embroidery on net. Embroidery on woven net was known as *buratto*, that on the more familiar knotted net as *lacis*. The design in both was developed by filling in squares of the mesh, somewhat like modern filet crochet. The background grid is very apparent in the finished piece.

Needlepoint laces developed from cutwork and drawnwork embroidery—techniques that involved removing or compressing the threads of the background fabric. As more and more fabric threads were removed, the more "lace-like" the work became. One of the first "true" laces to develop in this way was *reticella*, which consisted of filling in openings cut in the fabric with bars of buttonhole stitch. *Reticella* can be identified by its geometric structure.

With the appearance of *punto in aria*, literally, "stitches in the air," the background fabric disappeared completely. Instead, the design was traced onto parchment and outlined in thread. The stitches were then worked on the surface of the parchment over this thread framework. This technique allowed for much more freedom of design, and the geometric nature of the earlier laces soon disappeared. Later laces added raised cords and padding to the work, giving it a heavily textured, almost three-dimensional appearance. Perhaps the prime examples of this type of lace were the exquisite Venetian points produced in the seventeenth century.

Bobbin laces are more closely related to weaving. In this technique, the threads are wound onto bobbins—often hundreds for a single piece of lace—which are mounted on a pillow. The design is worked by interlacing the threads. Although Italy is best known for its needlepoint laces, many beautiful varieties of bobbin lace were also produced. Since the heavy needlepoint laces were so prized, it is not surprising that many of the bobbin laces imitated needlepoint lace patterns. When the fashion turned to lighter laces, however, bobbin lace became extremely popular and less dependent on needlepoint lace designs.

Of course, older styles did not disappear when new ones developed, and there is a great deal of overlap in the types of lace used. It is not at all unusual to find *lacis* designs imitating *punto in aria* and Venetian point laces with bobbin-lace edgings.

The photographs in this volume were selected from a rare two-volume work on Italian lace published in 1913. For this survey of Italian lace, the author, Elisa Ricci, searched out samples in museums and private collections throughout Europe and America.

Ricci has categorized needlepoint laces into four major divisions—*lacis* and related network, *reticella*, *punto in aria* and miscellaneous laces. Included under *punto in aria* are several laces that later lace historians would consider as separate classifications. We have generally kept Ricci's headings, although we have placed Venetian Point, Burano Point and Ivory Stitch in their own separate categories.

Bobbin laces are categorized according to where they were made, since each area developed its own style of lace.

These beautiful photographs should provide valuable information to the collector, inspiration for lacemakers, and a source of readily usable illustrations for graphic designers.

CONTENTS

1. Insertion in linen stitch with bobbin-lace edging, 16th century.   2–3. *Lacis* embroidered in various stitches, 17th century.

4. *Lacis* with linen openwork and *reticella*, 17th century.   5. Insertion embroidered with threads of different thickness, bobbin-lace edging, 17th century.

6

6. Alternating squares of linen stitch and matting stitch with triangles of *mezzo-mandolina*,
16th–17th century.

7. Insertion in linen stitch, darning stitch and matting stitch (imitating *reticella*), 17th century.

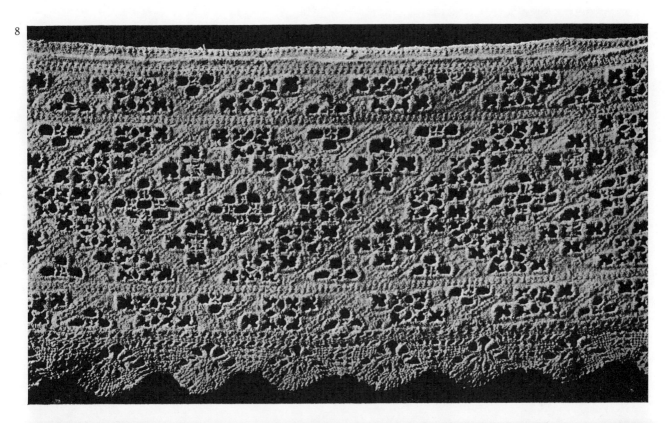

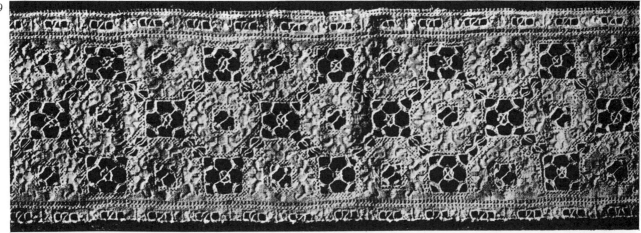

8. Insertion in *reticella* and cut linen, 16th century.   9. Insertion in satin stitch and *reticella*, 16th century.   10. Insertion in curl and satin stitch and *reticella*, 16th century.

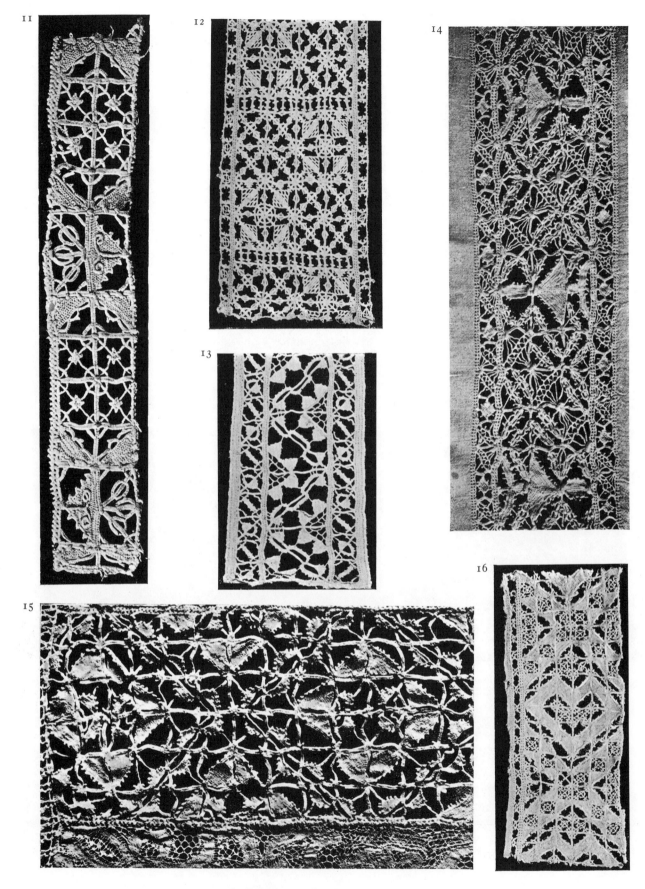

11–16. Cut linen and embroidery, 16th century.

17

18

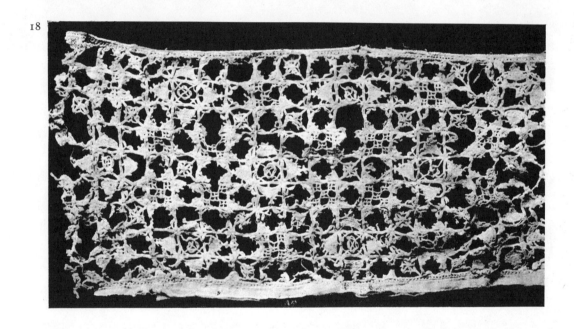

19

20

17–20. Insertions, 16th century.

21

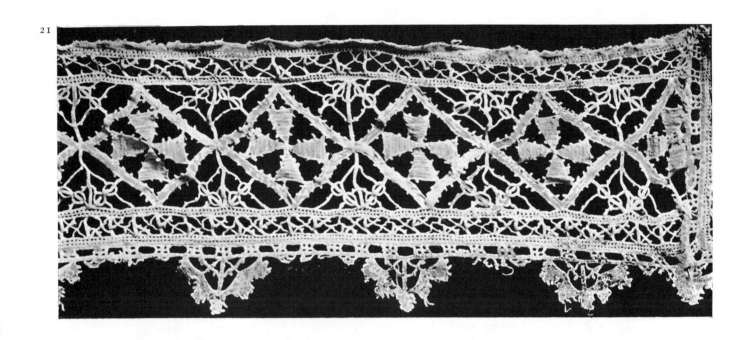

22

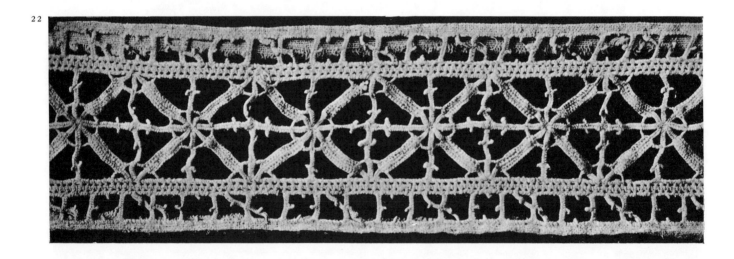

23

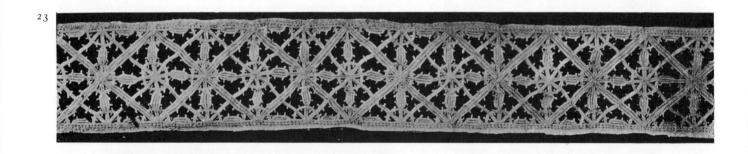

21–23. Insertions, 16th century.

24. Pillow slip in curl stitch and *reticella*, 16th century.

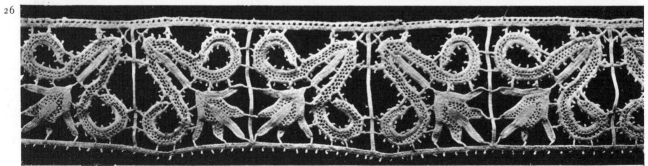

25. Tablecloth with bands and border of *reticella*, bobbin-lace edging, 16th century.
26. Insertion, 16th century.

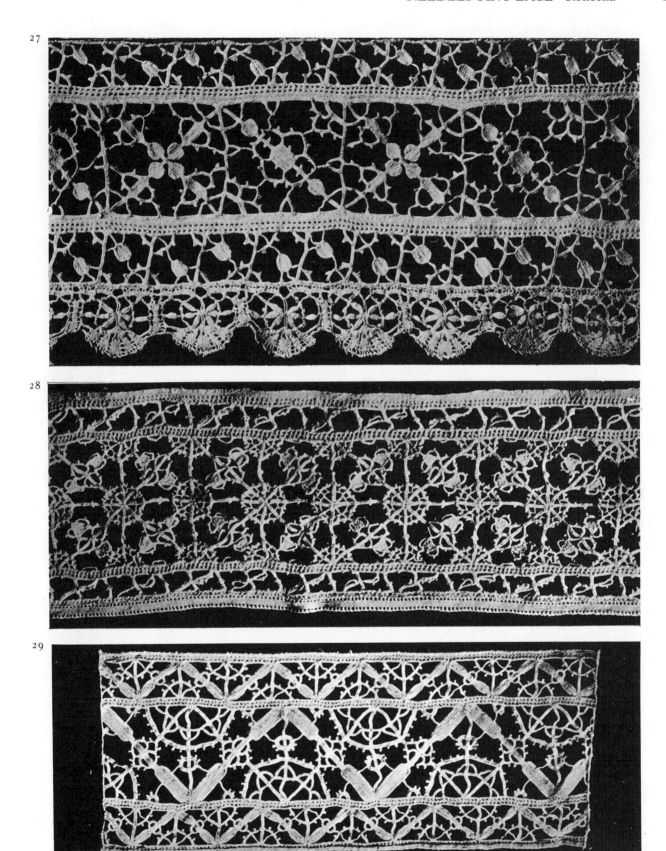

27–29. Insertions, 16th century.

30. Linen coverlet in curl stitch and *reticella*, bobbin-lace points, 16th century.

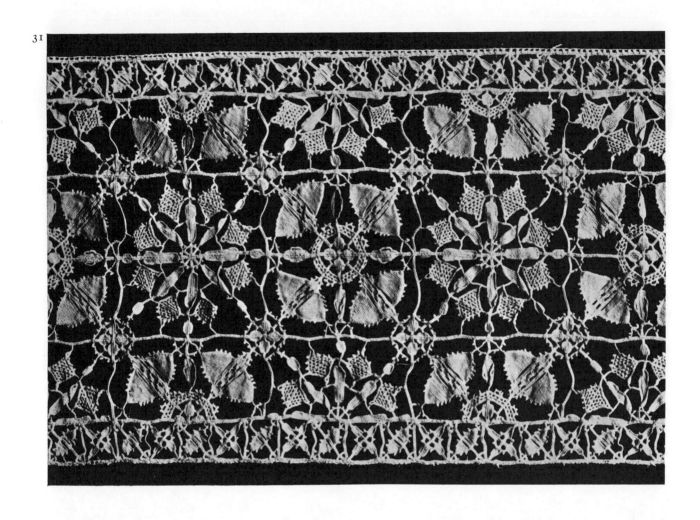

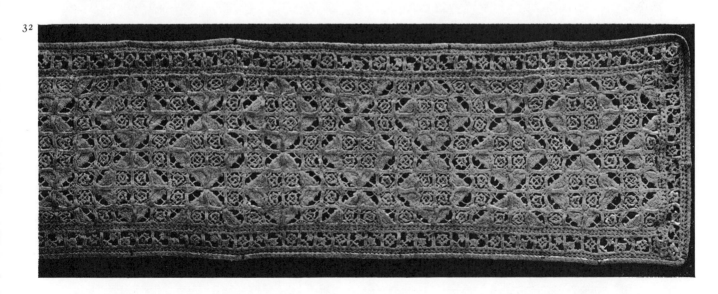

31. Insertion, 16th century.   32. Insertion in cut linen, 16th century.

33

34
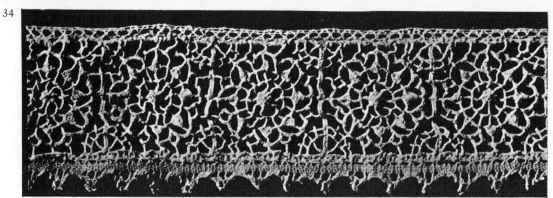

33. Squares, insertions and points of *reticella*, 16th century.   34. Insertion with bobbin-lace
edging, 16th century.

35. Insertion and points of *reticella*, 16th century.   36. Embroidery with curl and satin stitch and *reticella*, 16th century.

37

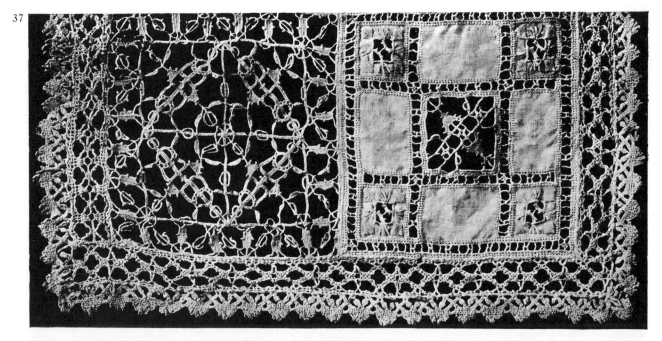

38

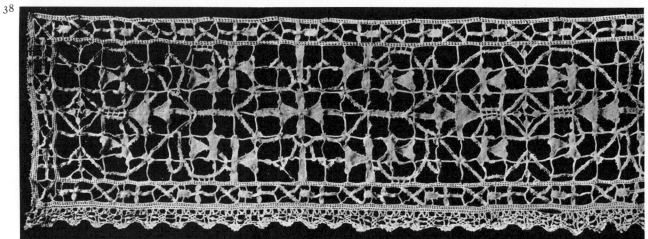

39

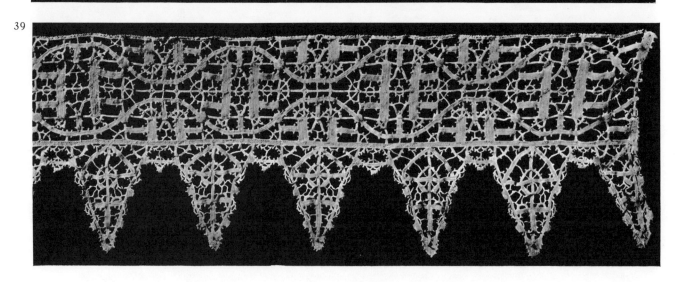

37. *Reticella* squares, 16th century.   38. Insertion, 16th century.   39. Insertion and points, 16th century.

40–42. Insertions, 16th century.   43. Insertion and edging, 16th century.

44

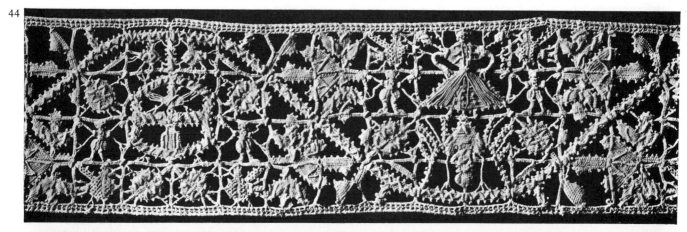

45

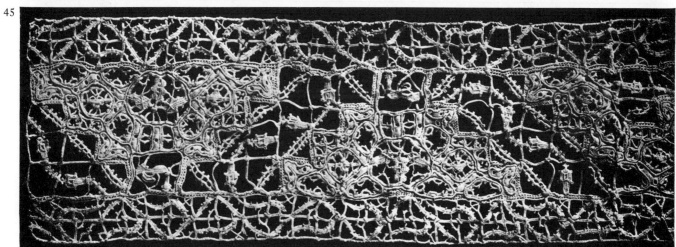

46

47

44. Insertion with a design in *punto in aria* on *reticella* network, 16th–17th century.
45. Insertion with embroidery in satin and curl stitch, 16th–17th century.   46–47. Insertions and edgings, 16th–17th century.

48

48. Tablecloth with *lacis* squares alternating with squares of pierced linen and *reticella*, 16th–
17th century.

49. *Reticella* insertion with edging of *punto in aria*, 16th–17th century.   50. Insertion and edging, 16th–17th century.   51. *Reticella* fragment with needle-made tassel, 16th–17th century.   52. Fragment in *reticella* and cut linen, 16th–17th century.   53. Edging, 16th–17th century.

54

54. Collar, 16th century

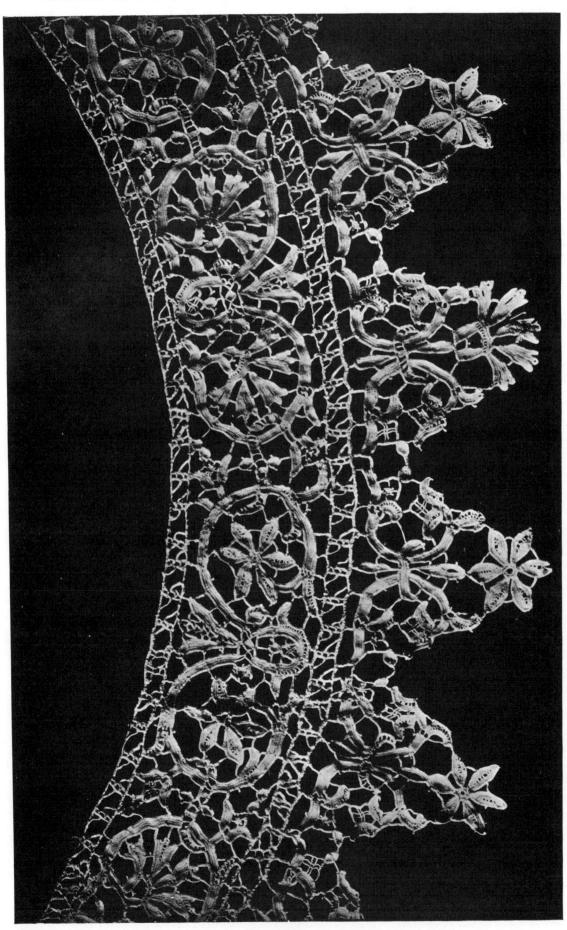

55. Collar, 16th century.

55

56. Apron with border and edging, 16th century.

56

57

57. Insertion with vertical design, 16th century.

58

58. Insertion with vertical design, 16th century.

59. Wide border and edging, 16th century.   60. Border and edging, 16th century.   61. Lace fragment, 16th century.   62. Edging, 16th century.

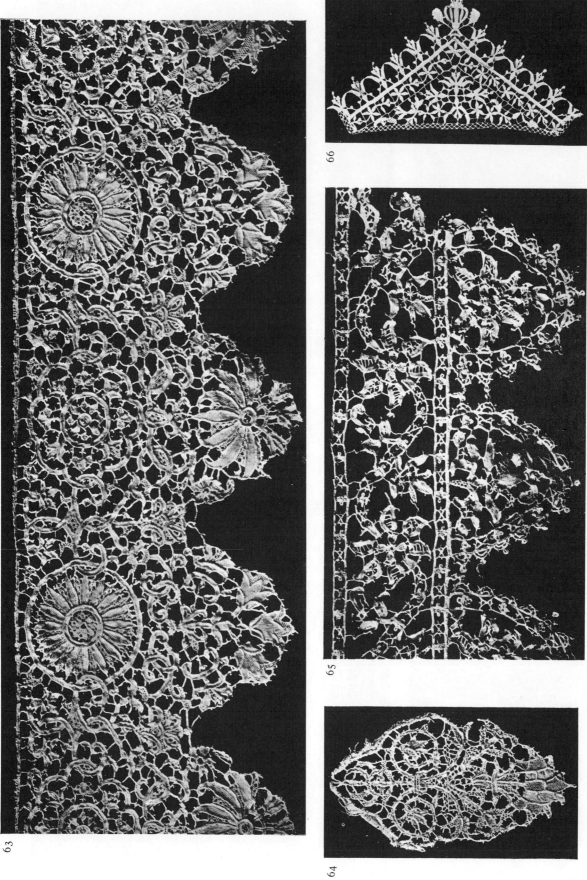

63. Edging, 16th century. 64. Lace fragment, 16th century. 65. Insertion and edging, 16th century. 66. Point for handkerchief, 16th century.

67–68. *Punto in aria* and embroidery, 16th century.

67

68

69. Lace with modern net foundation, 16th century.

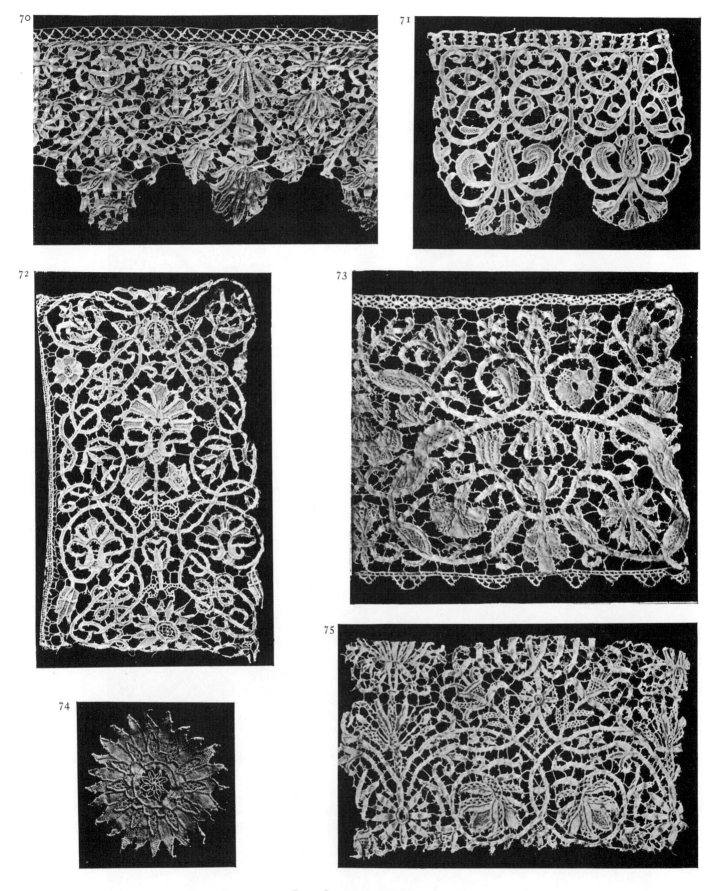

70–75. Lace fragments, 16th–17th century.

76

76. Insertion with vertical design, 16th century.

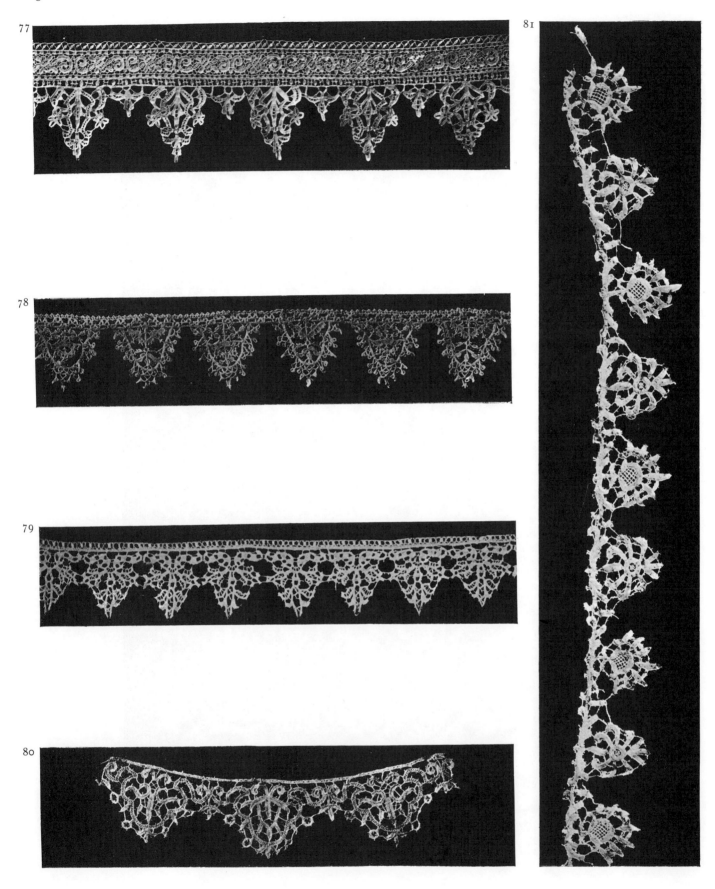

77–81. Edgings, 16th–17th century.

82

82. Alb trimming, 16th–17th century.

83

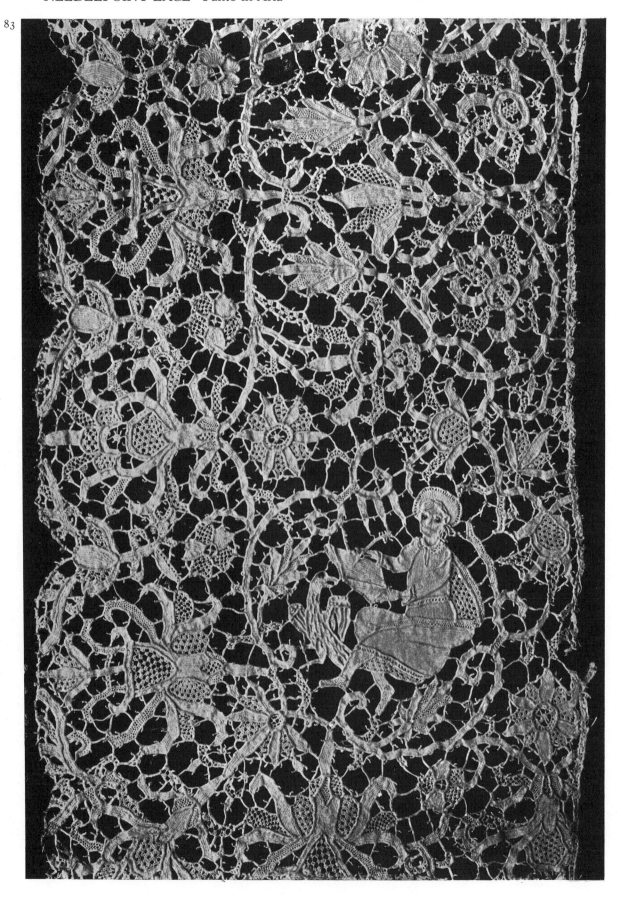

83. Alb trimming, 16th–17th century.

84

85

86

87

84–87. Isolated figures for insertion in groundwork of leaves and flowers, 17th century.

88. Collar, 17th century.

88

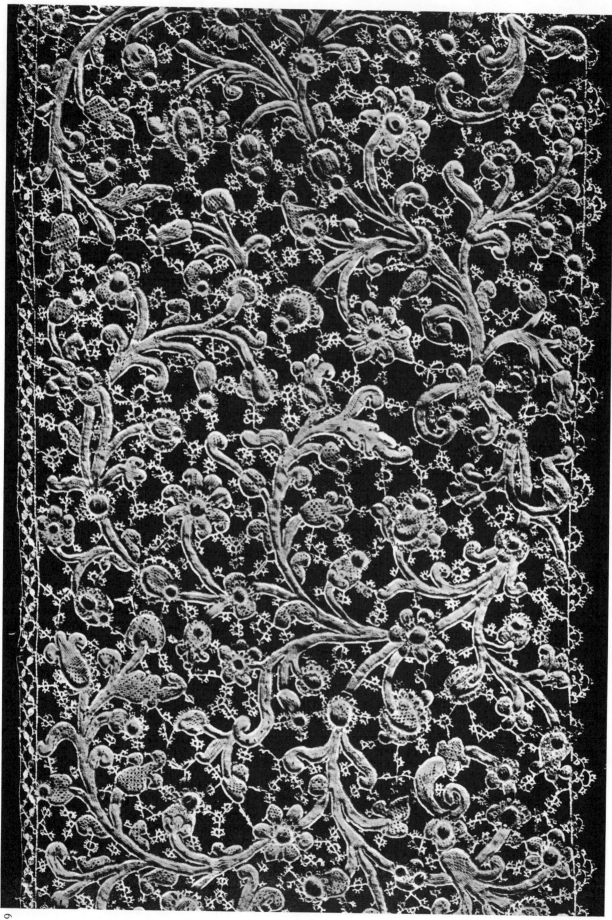

89. Heavy Venetian point with rosaline ground, 17th century.

90

91

90–91. Heavy Venetian point with tape and rosaline ground, 16th century.

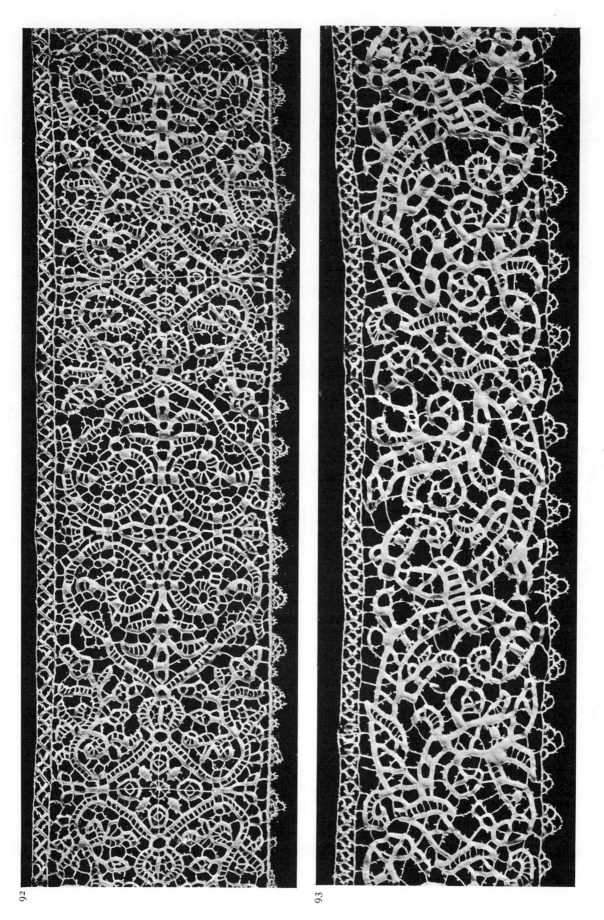

92–93. 17th century.

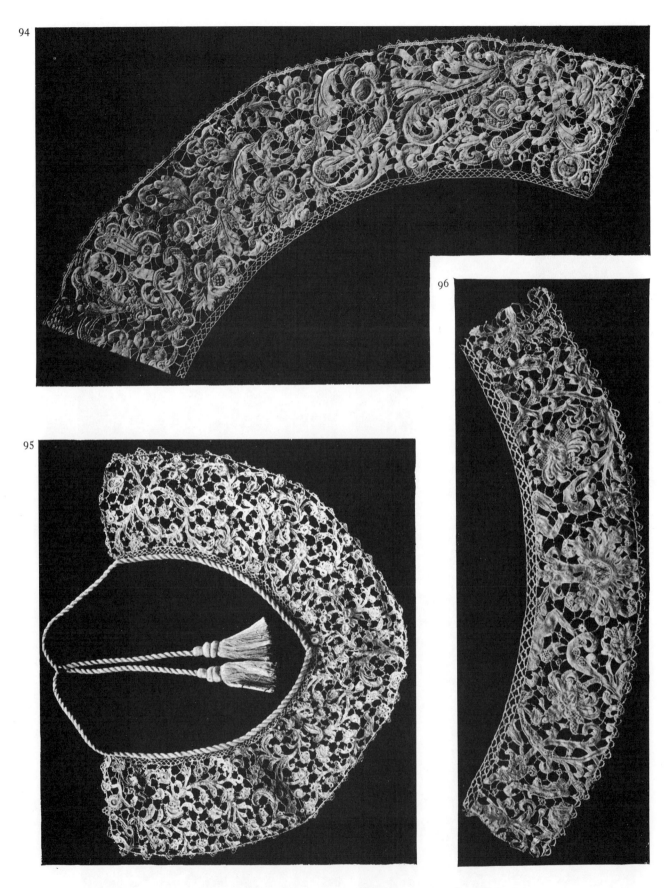

94–95. Collars, 17th century.   96. Fragment, 17th century.

97

98

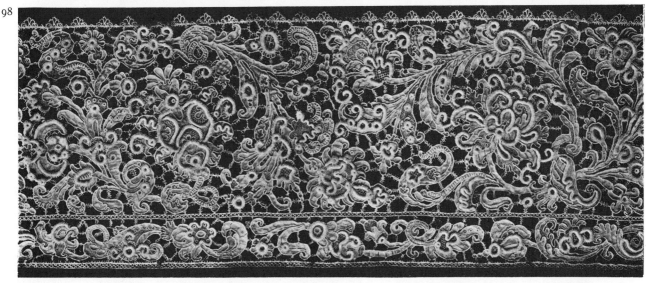

97. Votive cushion, 17th century.   98. Border, 17th century.

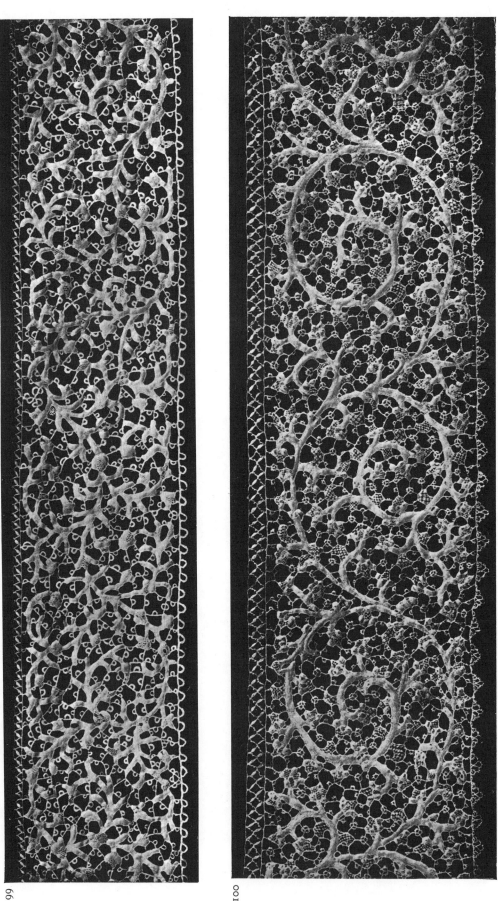

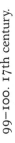

99–100. 17th century.

99

100

101. Heavy Venetian point with rosaline background, 17th century.

101

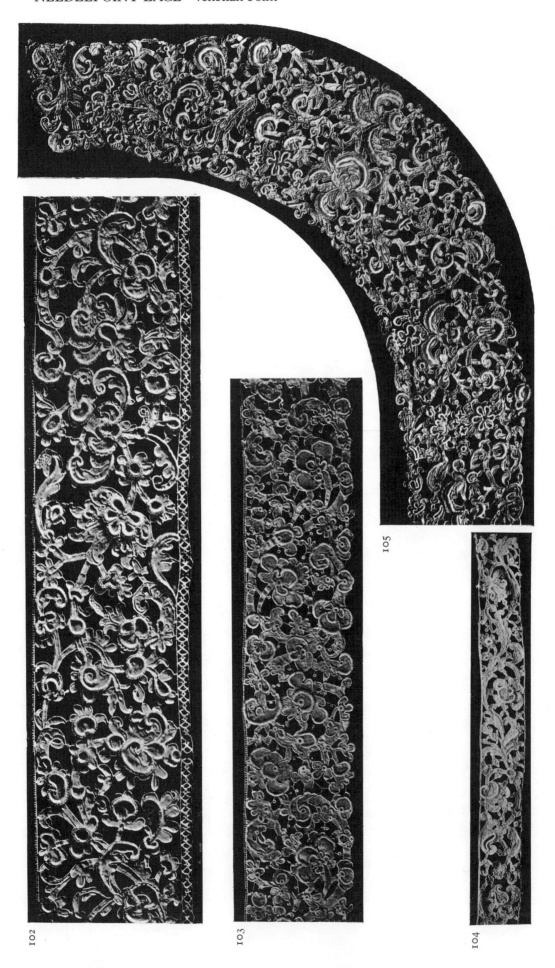

102

103

105

104

102. Insertion without background, 17th century. 103. Insertion, 17th century. 104. Insertion without background, 17th century. 105. 17th century.

106. 18th century.

107

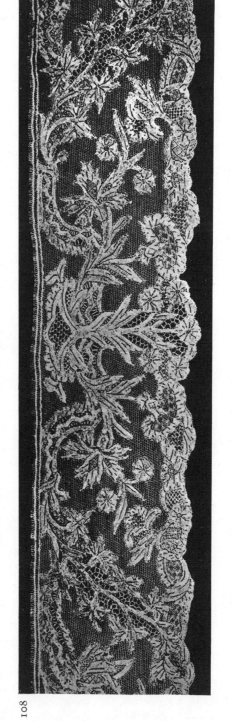

108

109

107–109. Venetian point with net foundation, imitating Flemish bobbin lace, 18th century.

110. Scarf made from design imitating French lace, 18th century.

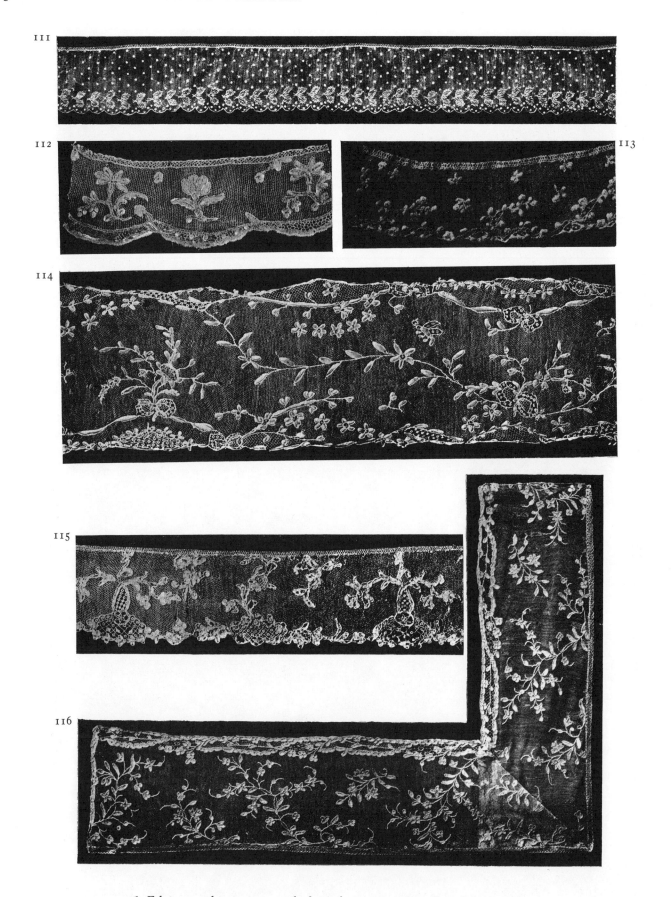

111–116. Edgings and insertions made from designs imitating French lace, 18th century.

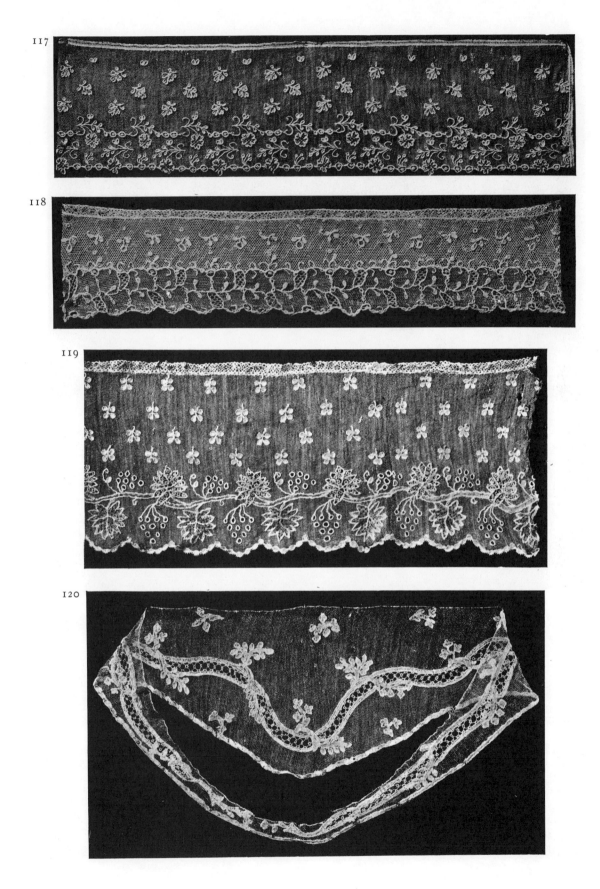

117–120. Edgings and insertions made from designs imitating Alençon lace, 18th century.

121. Collar from a design for *reticella*, 17th century.   122–123. Insertions from designs for
reticella, 17th century.

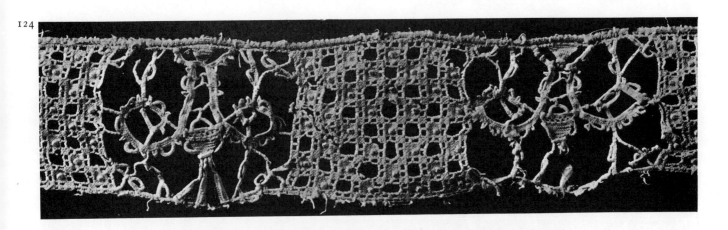

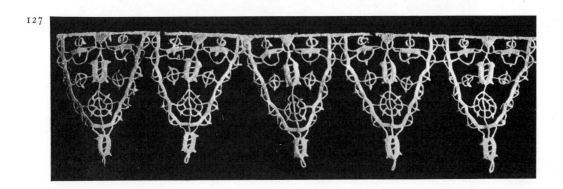

124. Insertion with alternate squares of ivory stitch and *punto in aria*, 17th century.   125–
126. Edgings, 17th century.   127. Edging from a design for *punto in aria*, 17th century.

128

129

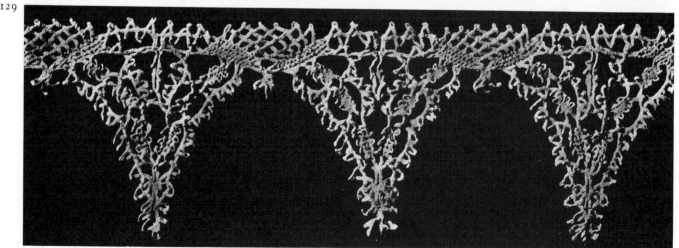

128. Insertion and edging, 16th century.   129. Points without selvage, 16th century.

130–133. Insertions similar to designs shown in *Le Pompe* (Venice, 1557), 16th century.

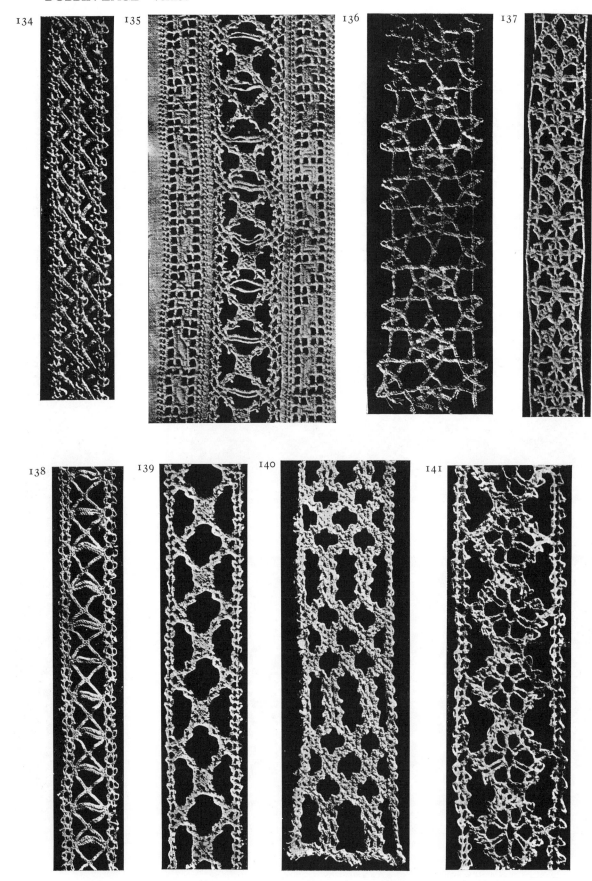

134–141. Insertions similar to designs shown in *Le Pompe* (Venice, 1557), 16th century.

142–149. Insertions, 16th century.

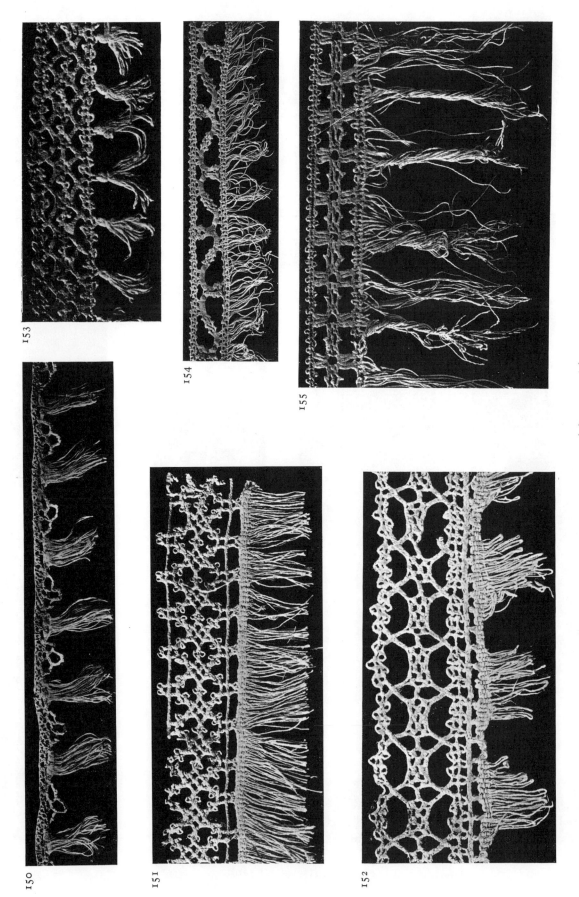

150–155. Insertions and fringes, 16th century.

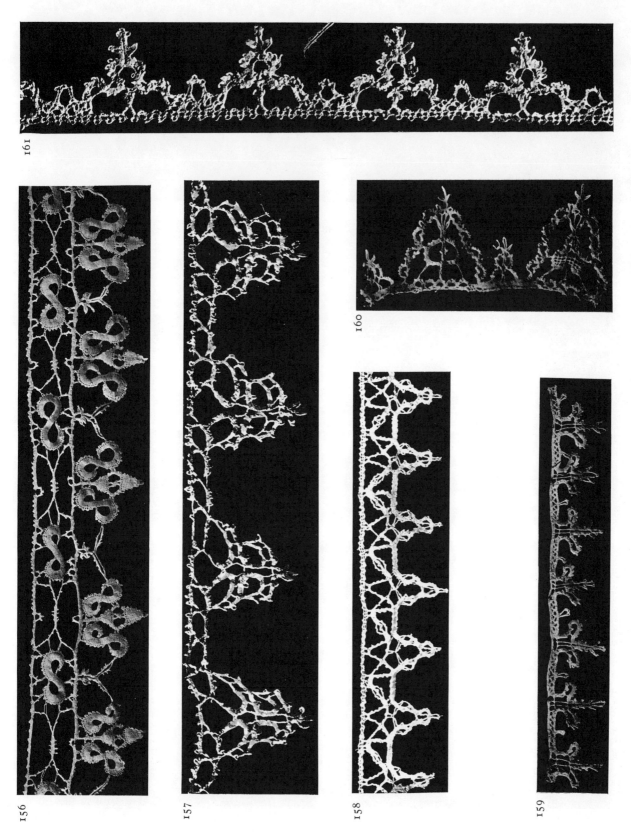

156. Insertion and edging, 16th–17th century.   157. Edging from a design for *punto in aria*, 16th–17th century.   158–159. Edgings, 16th–17th century.   160. Edging from design for *punto in aria*, 16th–17th century.   161. Edging, 16th–17th century.

162

163

164

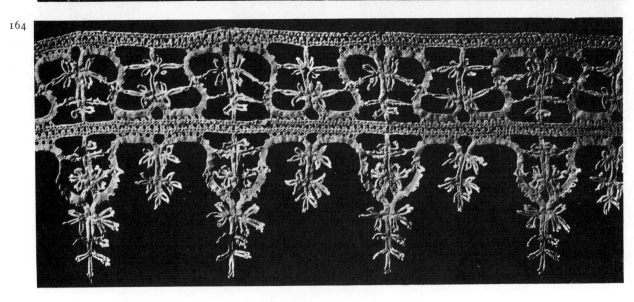

162–164. Insertions and edgings, 17th century.

165

166

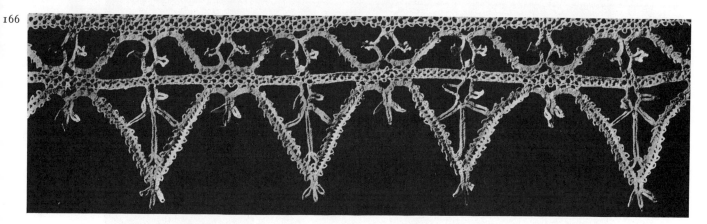

165–166. Insertions and edgings, 16th–17th century.

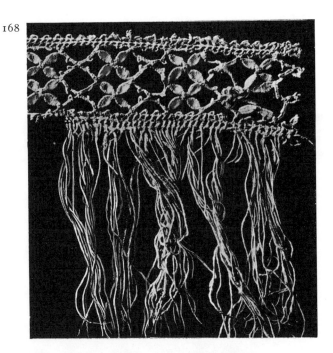

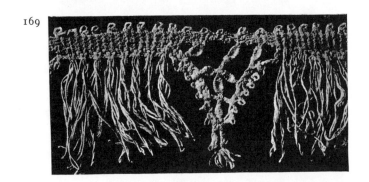

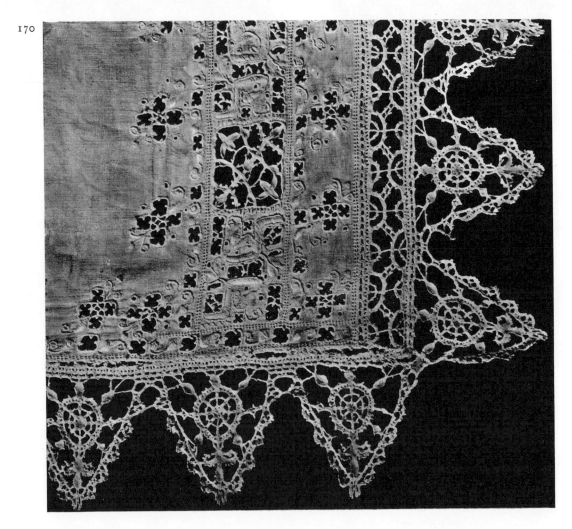

167. Insertion from a *reticella* design, 16th century.   168–169. Fringes and insertions from *reticella* designs, 16th century.   170. Tablecloth with bobbin-lace insertion and edging taken from *reticella* design, 16th century.

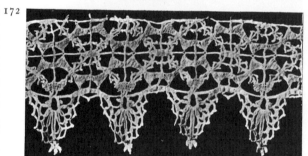

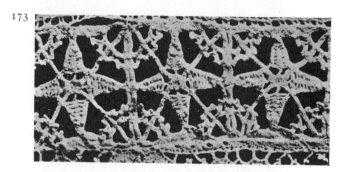

171–174. Insertions and edgings from designs for *punto tagliato* (cut linen), 16th century.

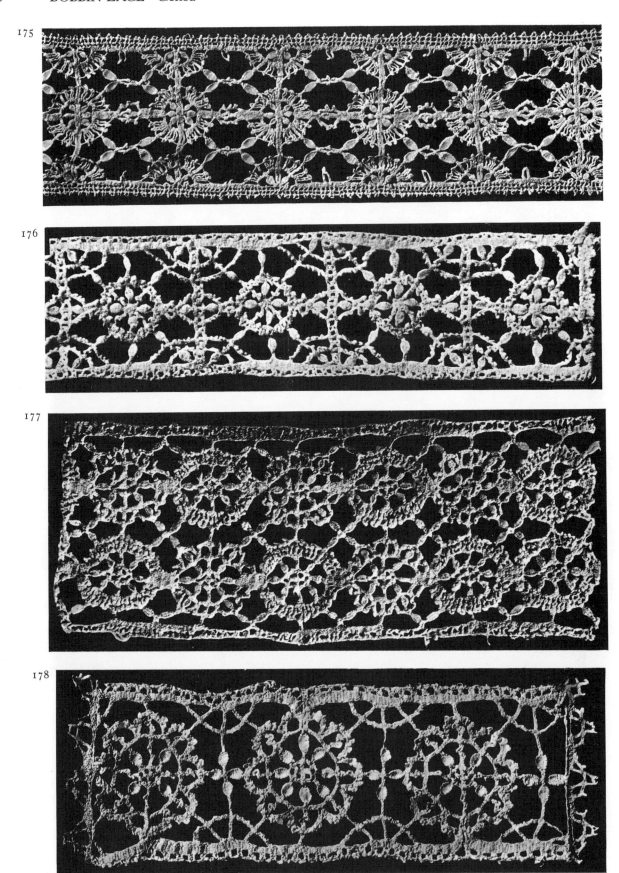

175–178. Insertions with variations on a single design for *reticella*, 16th century.

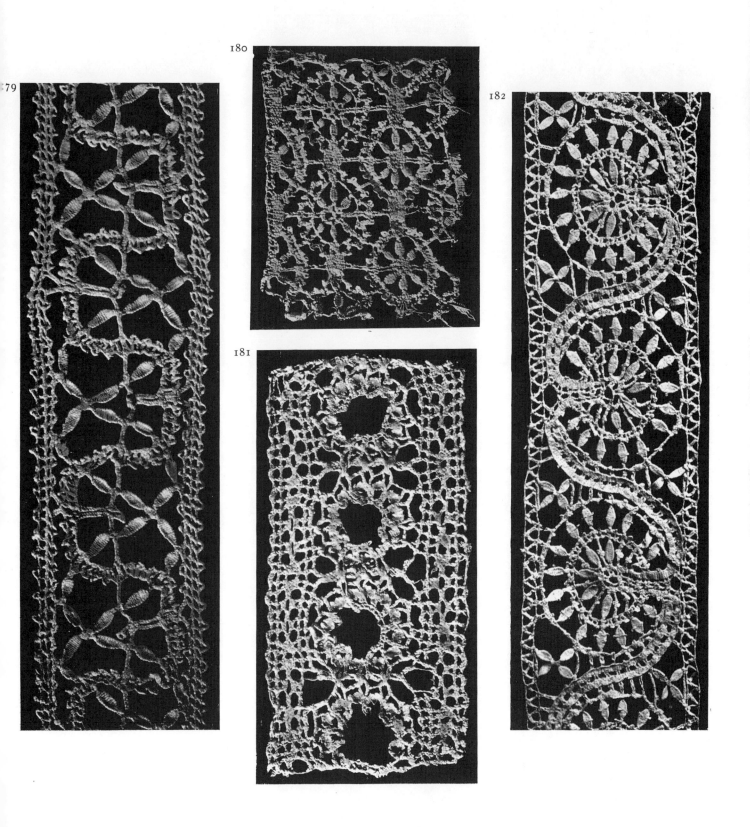

179–182. Insertions, 17th century.

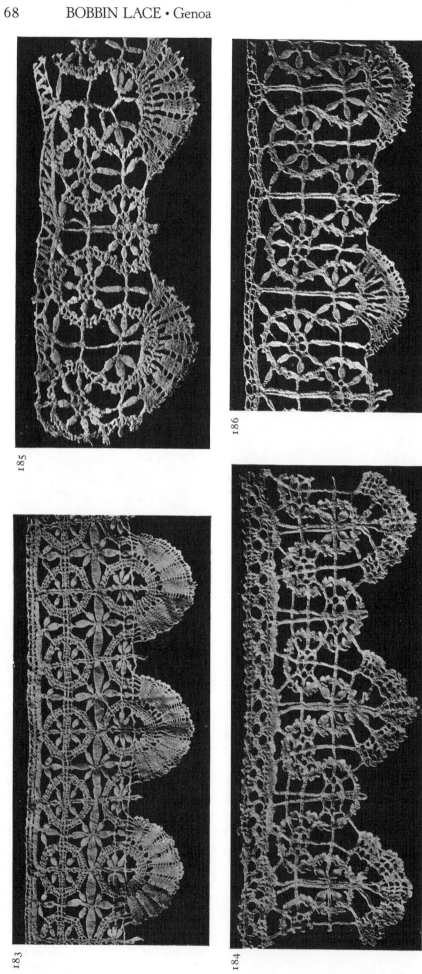

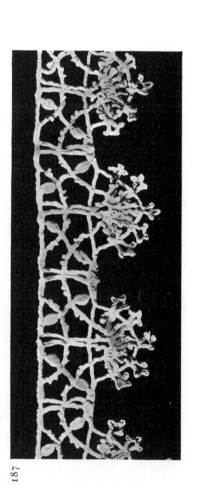

183–187. Edgings with bell points, 17th century.

188. Pinafore with insertion and edging from a design for *punto in aria*, 17th century.

189

190

191

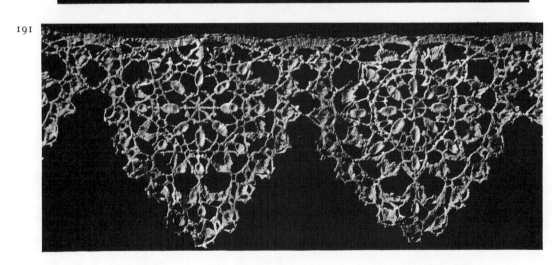

189–191. Genoese rose-lace edgings, 17th century.

192

193

194

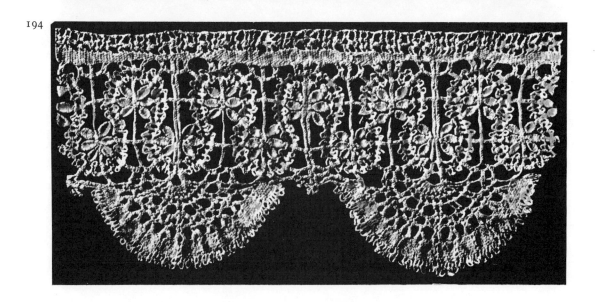

192–194. Genoese rose-lace edgings with bell points, 17th century.

195–198. Genoese rose-lace edgings, 17th century.

199. Pointed edging from a design for *punto in aria*, 17th century.

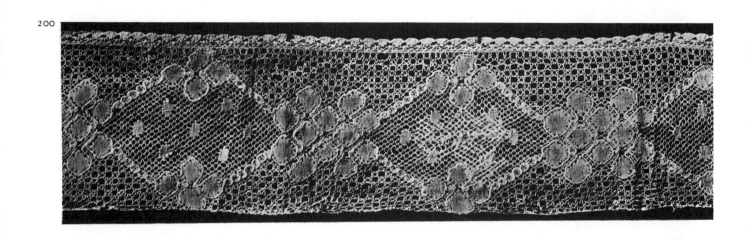

200–202. Ligurian imitations of foreign laces, 18th century.

203–209. Ligurian edgings imitating foreign laces, 18th–19th century.

210

211

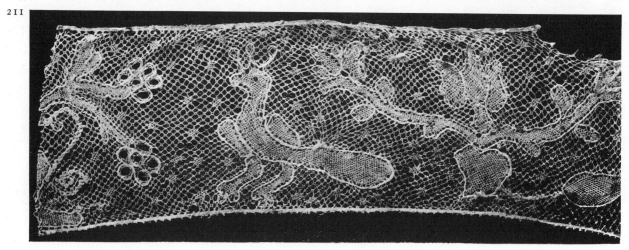

210–211. Ligurian imitations of Mechlin lace, 18th century.

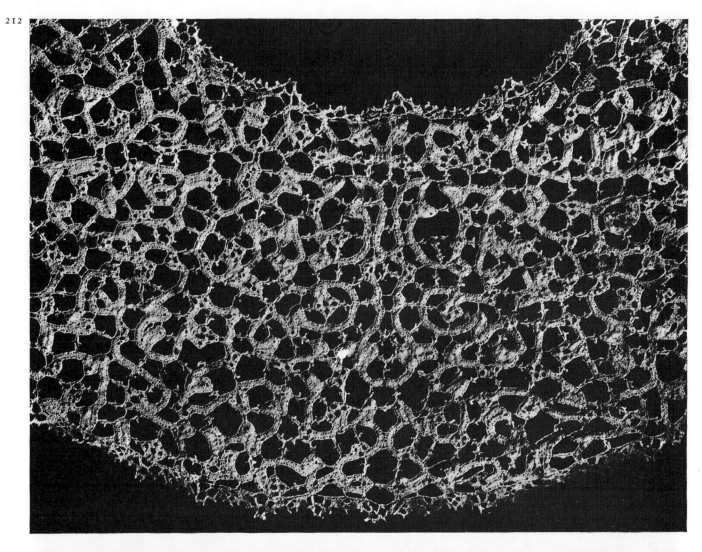

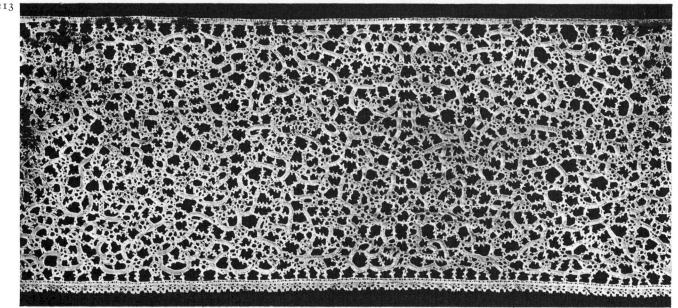

212–213. Lace with spiral design and continuous braid, 16th–17th century.

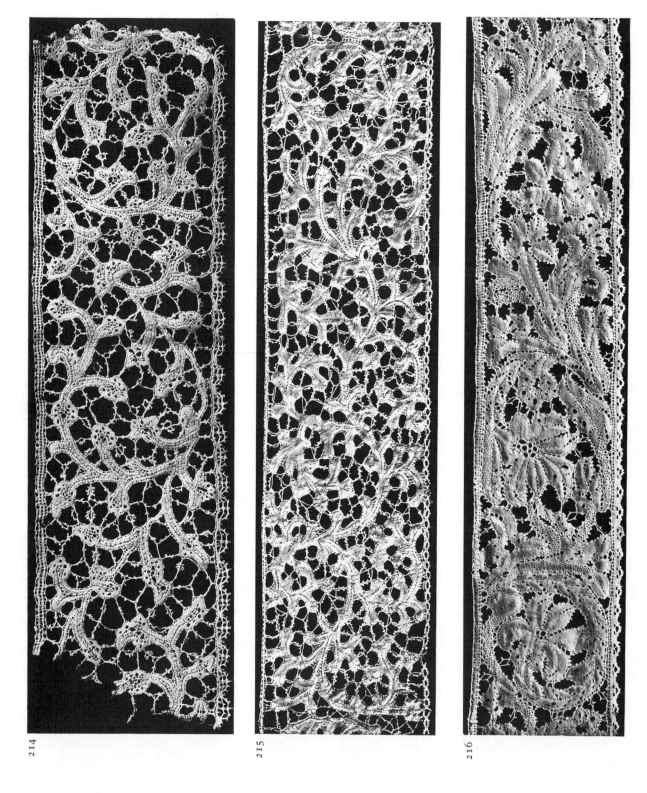

214

215

216

214–216. Lace with continuous braid design, 16th–17th century.

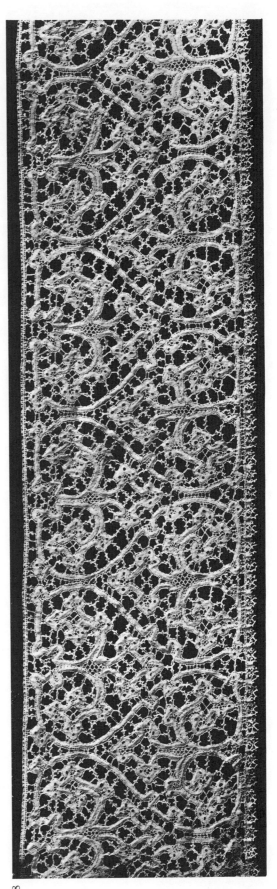

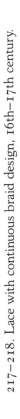

217

218

217–218. Lace with continuous braid design, 16th–17th century.

219. Alb trimming with continuous braid, 17th century.

220. Alb trimming with continuous braid and various openwork designs, 17th century.

220

221. Lace for high wired collar, 17th–18th century.

222. Lace with two foundations, 17th–18th century.

223

224

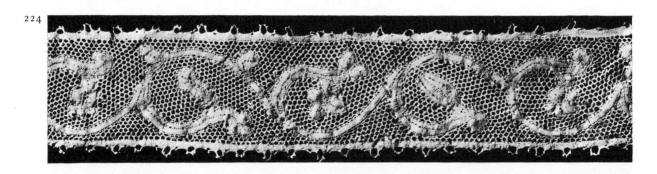

225

223. Figured lace on net foundation, 17th–18th century.   224–225. Lace with continuous
braid on a foundation, 17th–18th century.

226

226. Fragment of insertion, probably the corner of an altar cloth, 18th century.

227

227. 18th century.

228

228. Insertion with vertical design, 18th century.

229. Alb trimming with hunting motifs, 18th century.

230. Alb trimming, 18th century.

230

231
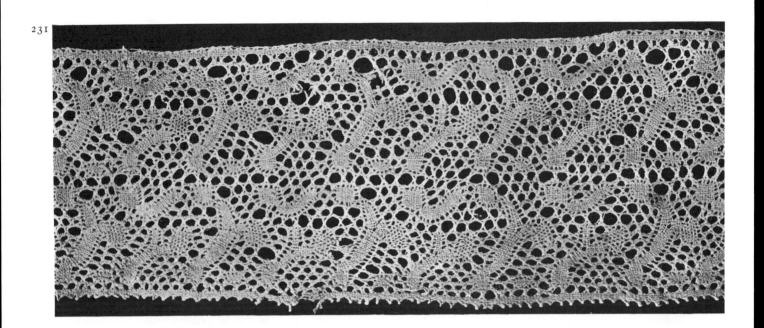

232
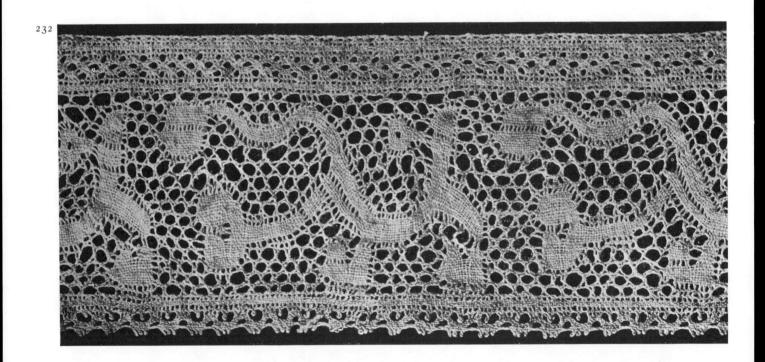

231–232. Insertions, 17th century.

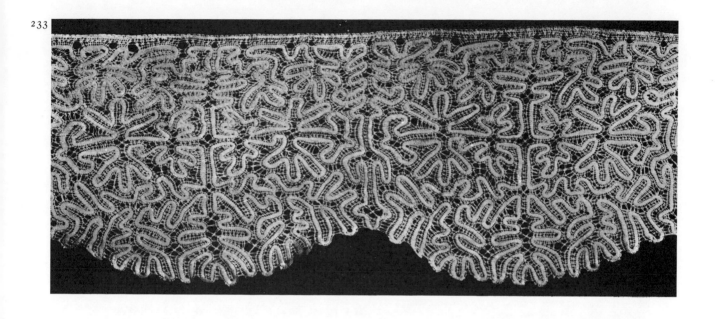

233–234. Alb trimmings with continuous braid; Aquila, 17th century.

235

236

235. Towel with *lacis* insertions and macramé border, 16th century.   236. Border of bobbin lace, *lacis*, *reticella*, drawn thread and colored embroidery with macramé insertion and edging, 16th century.

237
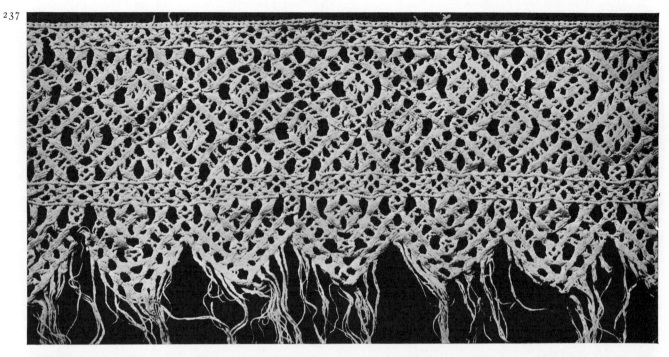

238
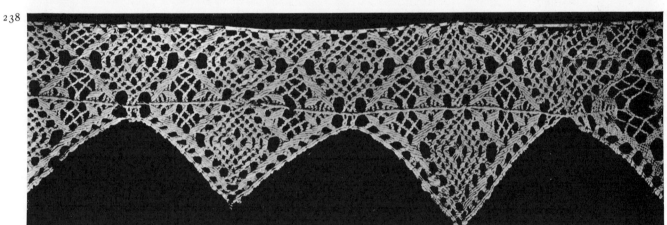

239
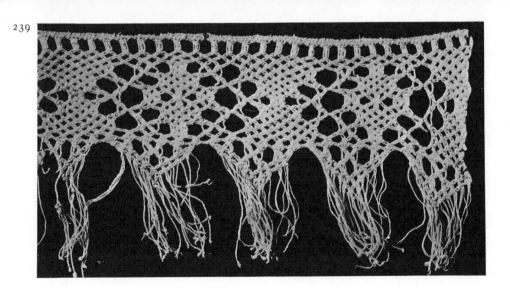

237. Wide border and edging with macramé fringe, 16th century. 238. Wide border and edging, 16th century. 239. Wide border and edging with macramé fringe, 16th century.

240

241

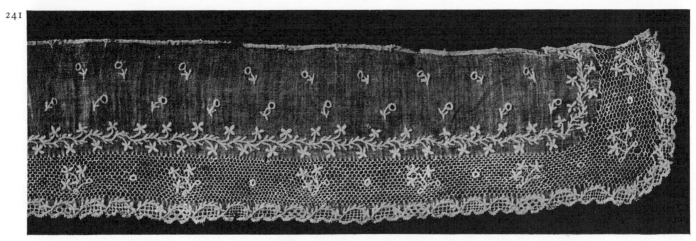

240–241. Drawn thread on very fine linen, imitating needlepoint lace, 18th century.

242. Crochet work from a bobbin-lace design, 19th century.   243. Crochet work imitating
Venetian point, 19th century.